Scale Studies for the Third Octave for the Cello, Book Two, by Cassia Harvey

CHP210

©2012 by C. Harvey Publications All Rights Reserved.

www.charveypublications.com - print books
www.Learnstrings.com - PDF downloadable books
www.harveystringarrangements.com - chamber music

Scale Studies for the Third Octave, for the Cello

1

Book Two

Cassia Harvey

Note: The scales studied in this book are listed at the end.

©2012 C. Harvey Publications All Rights Reserved.

2

Scale Studies for the Third Octave, for the Cello, Book Two

3

4

Scale Studies for the Third Octave, for the Cello, Book Two

5

©2012 C. Harvey Publications All Rights Reserved.

6

7

8

9

10

11

12

13

14

Scale Studies for the Third Octave, for the Cello, Book Two

15

16

17

18

19

20

21

22

Scale Studies for the Third Octave, for the Cello, Book Two

23

24

Scale Studies for the Third Octave, for the Cello, Book Two

25

Scale Studies for the Third Octave, Book Two

If you have difficulty finding the starting note
for exercises 26-36, play this first:

26

©2012 C. Harvey Publications All Rights Reserved.

27

28

29

30

31

32

33

34

35

Also play this exercise slurred,
with one measure in a bow.

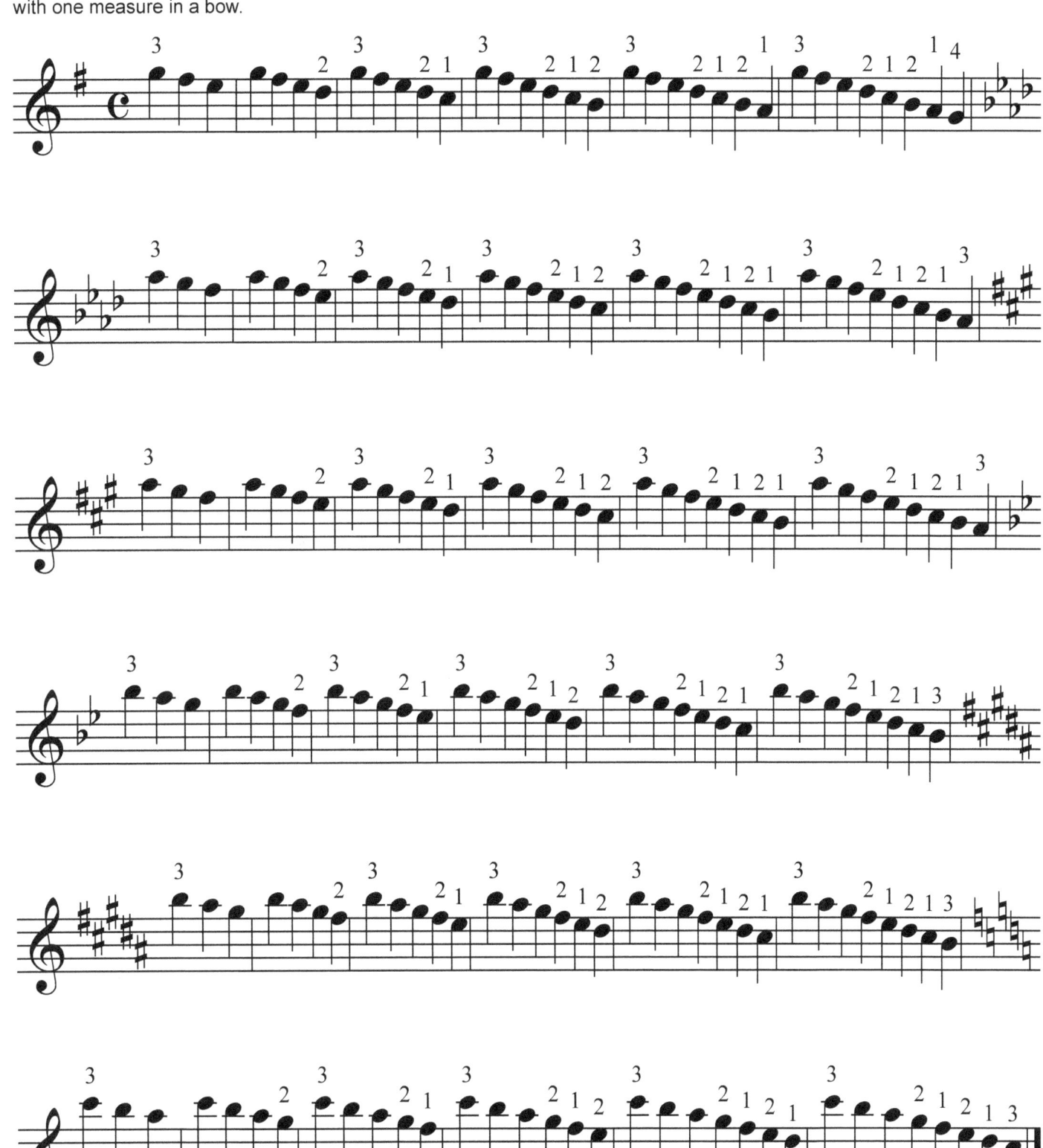

36

37

38

39

40

41

42

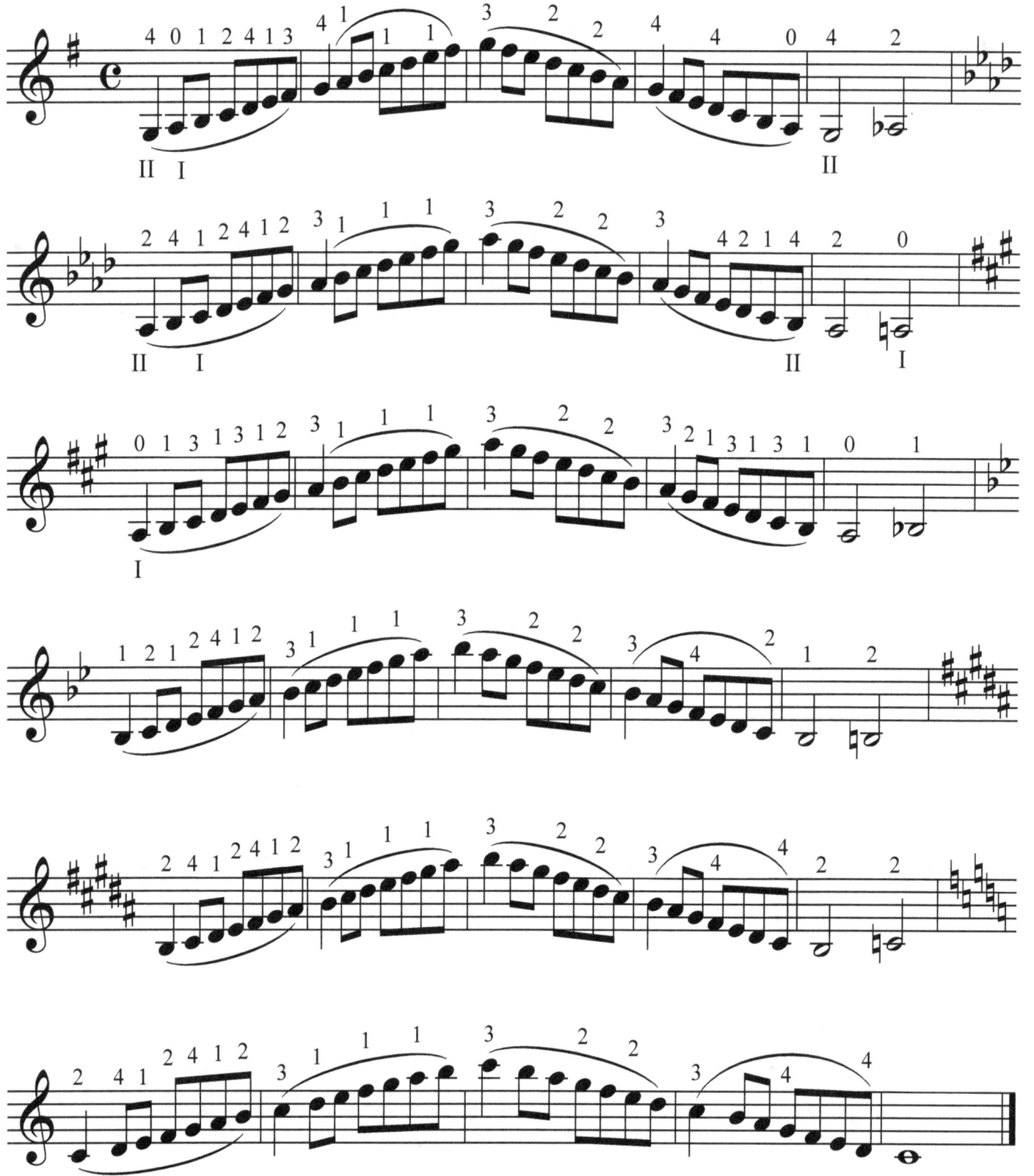

Scale Studies for the Third Octave, for the Cello, Book Two

Scale Studies for the Third Octave, Book Two

B♭ major (flats: B and E)

B major (sharps: F, C, G, D, and A)

C major: 4 octaves!

©2012 C. Harvey Publications All Rights Reserved.

www.ingramcontent.com/pod-product-compliance
Lightning Source LLC
Chambersburg PA
CBHW081734100526
44591CB00016B/2617